Life

*Key to your soul...
a journey into the Self*

Letters

ALYSHIA OCHSE

ISBN 978-0-9862468-0-7

Printed in the United States of America.

10 9 8 7 6 5 4 3 2 1

This book is
dedicated to
YOU.

THIS
WAY
IN

Awakening 2
Invitation 6
Transformation...8
Innovation 10
The Greater Source 26
Celebration 28
Inspiration 30
Gratitude 48

Yes, this is a self-help book,
but it is not your typical self-help book.
It is only a few pages long so that
you can get to the focus of your quest:

evolution of self.

This book is designed to give you the monthly tools
to continue to evolve into
the person you imagine yourself to be.
It is short and simple—

quite possibly the shortest book you'll get the most out of.

If you don't want to procrastinate any longer,
this is the book for you.
Trust me, this one will work
and will keep on giving for the whole year.

awakening

I t all started with a lunch menu. *What did I want for lunch? Salad? Sandwich?* I didn't know. At that time, I no longer had a partner to ask anymore. Being alone wasn't a problem. The issue I found myself grappling with, while standing in line to order some food, was that I didn't know what I liked at 28 years old. An even big-ger problem, and here came my meltdown, was that I didn't know who I was. For 28 years, I'd had parents, siblings, coaches, teachers, friends, society, and, lately, a fiancé helping me make decisions and form hobbies for ... me. *But what did I want? What did I like? What do I do? Salad. Sandwich. Salad. Sandwich. Was I even hungry?* Honestly, I had no idea which one I actually liked more. I ordered both.

From this point forward, I would be ordering both of many things. I had recently called off my wedding—three months before the Big Day, "save the dates" already sent, dress already picked out. I thought he didn't "get" me, so how could I marry him? In his defense, *I* didn't get me ... *so how could he marry me?* Huge realization in retrospect. I was looking for answers. Specifically, I was looking for someone else to give me the answers. I was so disconnected from myself that I didn't know which way to turn. So I took what was to be my honeymoon adventure and instead traveled with my best friend. Surely Egypt and Greece would have the answers I was seeking. On the plane ride there, I figured it out. I would write a letter to my ex-fiancé explaining who I am and why I do the things I do. That was it. It was settled. I would write a letter every day. Greece would give me the inspiration to write these letters and it would all be better. After all, I was not giving up on the future I had deemed was my destiny.

But in Greece, I grew depressed and angry. Here I was, on my "pseudo-honeymoon" and I felt sick to my stomach. Nothing was coming to me, and nothing felt right. *How could I explain who I am if I didn't know?* My friend and I decided to hike Mt. Sinai when we arrived in Egypt. We both thought that if Moses found the Ten Commandments at the top of this mountain, God would bestow upon us divine wisdom at this same site. We began up the steep slope at nightfall. Shooting stars whizzed past as we grew dizzy from the climb. I barely spoke, and my thoughts consumed me. *Why? Why? Why is this happening? What am I supposed to do? Tell me, please. I'm listening. I'm just here, waiting for a cue.* We arrived at the top of the mountain, and there it was, clear as could be in the night sky. A perfect constellation in the form of a question mark. I glanced at my best friend. "Do you see what I see?" She did. And then we laughed. I finally laughed. The laugh that woke up my soul. The answer to my question was ... a question mark.

> **Why? Why? Why is this happening? What am I supposed to do? Tell me, please. I'm listening. I'm just here, waiting for a cue.**

Either my subconscious had a wicked sense of humor, or whoever was playing my cards upstairs was having the night off. Alas, another day was steadily approaching and the only thing that was different now was that I finally "let go." I couldn't fight any longer. I couldn't look for the answers any harder. I gave up and enjoyed the peace of the sun rising over the mountains.

What goes up, must come down, literally. We had to hike back down the damn mountain. I was terrified. *Did I mention I am afraid of heights?* The heights issue hadn't occurred to me the night before because I had been consumed with my thoughts and the darkness protected me. Now, with the sun shining, I was looking at a drop down for miles. One slip and there would be no more questions. Ironic, isn't it? In the darkness, I had trust. In the light, I had fear. I was coming down with no answers, but I didn't have it in me anymore. Finally, I surrendered. I took a deep breath and exhaled my anxiety. Then, clear as someone talking to me, I had the thought: *I NEED the letters. The letters are for me. I need to understand me. I need to know ME.*

"I NEED the letters.
The letters are for me.
I need to understand me.
I need to know ME."

invitation

With an experience of solitude I derived *Life Letters*—letters that have given (and continue to give) me a monthly focus on exploring who I am and what fascinates me. With these letters I derived self-love, and with love I found forgiveness, acceptance, and excitement. *Life Letters* is a guide to diving inside one's inner self rather than searching for meaning and answers solely via external sources. It's an influential, different approach to understanding one's self through monthly adventures. The letters are a practice of teaching yourself how to be "healthily selfish," so to speak, and grow into the fullest form of your soul's request. It is learning how to take care of yourself fully from the inside out, relinquishing feelings of being ashamed of anything that represents YOU. *Life Letters* is the beginning of embracing your uniqueness and exploring all that life has to offer.

> **With these letters I derived self-love, and with love I found forgiveness, acceptance and excitement.**

Consider this book an instructional tool to access your inner self and continue to evolve. My belief is that everything will, and does, come from within. Therefore, in order for one not to become dependent on an exterior source for happiness or guidance, I've kept these instructions brief and simple. Understanding your desires, motives, and composition is simple. It is about making the time for yourself and no longer making excuses that keep you disconnected from your soul or inner guidance. I encourage you to begin this journey as soon as possible. Let's not prolong the discoveries that are waiting for you.

transformation

[In-ti-ma-cy: Into me YOU see]

ow many times have you said "I love you" to a friend, lover, family member, or even a virtual stranger? How many times have you said "I love you" to yourself? You are what you think. Thoughts develop into beliefs, beliefs inform action. What would happen if you actually loved yourself?

You will be instructed to write "I love you" at the end of each monthly letter. It might seem like an uncomfortable exercise, but when you state it and read it each month the phrase will begin to lose its bashful sentiments and actually become sincere. To write it, to read it, to say it, to think it, and then to believe it all are steps to it becoming your new reality. In human nature we usually find it very easy to love others but challenging to love ourselves. Most of us criticize an individual for self-love. Others may judge or be negative, solely on the basis of lacking their own self-love. But this is about you, your preservation of self, and your desires that create the individual that you are. In seeking love for yourself, you will see a graciousness that will allow the light of your world to shine from the inside to touch those around you. Self-forgiveness will come easier, patience for your weaknesses will strengthen, and acceptance of the world's view of you will become less of a priority. What makes you YOU will be celebrated through self-love. Give to yourself what you so readily give to others: intimacy and love.

> **...this is about you, your preservation of self, and your desires that create the individual that you are.**

You can control how that love is appreciated and respected. Only positive thoughts and actions should surround the idea of self-love, yet as a society we often scold, criticize, or neglect to celebrate someone for loving themselves. Instead of following those thoughts, I challenge them and therefore challenge you to see what will happen when you start to express love for yourself through thoughts, actions, and speech. Start with the thought, write it down, and read it to yourself every month.

innovation

The first rule of my guidance is to be truly honest with yourself. There are no benefits in hiding behind what you think will benefit you or what you think will impress others. You know why you were attracted to this guidance, and you sense what your soul desires. Just listen and proceed without judgment. Which brings me to my second rule: **no judgments!**

Items you will need for the next steps:

1) Notebook paper
2) Pen
3) Twelve envelopes
4) Special box

Step 1

 Evaluate your supposed limitations, regrets, or that which you lack.

Spend some time with yourself with no interactions with others or distractions from the outside world. Evaluate your past year or your full past, if you must. Only spend a half hour in this nostalgic period. Go through regrets, mistakes, and desires that were not acknowledged or fully embraced. Write them down. Be objective and mindful that this is just an evaluation to derive the opposite of that which you feel you lack. **This exercise is meant to stimulate what you desire to change.**

EXAMPLE: *Horrible with money, haven't traveled, hate my clothes, haven't read a book, don't know how to sew, have a bad relationship with my siblings, want a child, didn't get the promotion, hate my job, only speak one language, house is messy, haven't finished my book, bite my nails, horrible friend, no holiday traditions.*

Step 1: Evaluation

Feel free to use your own notebook paper or this space for your thoughts.

Step 2

Brainstorm the opposite.

Okay, now STOP the first step. For the next half hour write down ideas, topics, desires that interest you, the "you" you want to become or fully embrace. What would the opposite word or thought be of your limitations or regrets? Brainstorm. Doodle. Imagine. Don't hold back. **Go for everything and anything!** Write down anything that evokes emotion for you to truly become that person you have always wanted to be or knew you should be. For example:

be more CONFIDENT

Join book club

save money!

start a project

TRAVEL

go back to school

Marriage

start a blog

great abs!

NEW JOB

learn to knit

art class

beautiful skin

garden

learn to cook

exercise MORE

visit NYC

music

bake more often

Step 2: Brainstorm

Feel free to use your own notebook paper or this space for your thoughts.

Step 3

Pick twelve.

Circle twelve things out of your brainstorm that you want to focus on this year. Make a list numbered one through twelve, and next to each number, in no particular order, write one word that embraces that thought, desire, or action. You will have more time later on to elaborate on each topic. For example:

Step 3: List twelve

Feel free to use your own notebook paper or this space for your list.

1) _____

2) _____

3) _____

4) _____

5) _____

6) _____

7) _____

8) _____

9) _____

10) _____

11) _____

12) _____

Write your letters.

To each person, each of the aforementioned topics might mean something different. In that manner, we are already exploring and celebrating the uniqueness of everyone. Your list can be things that you have always wanted to do, things that you haven't done as well as you liked, and/or topics that you have always wanted to understand or discuss.

You will need twelve pieces of paper. I prefer paper with lines, but you might want to use unlined and/or colored paper; choose whatever makes you happy. Pick one of your twelve words. On one piece of paper write a letter to yourself about what you would like to explore regarding that topic. Have your letter only be one side of the page and center just on one of the words/topics that you have written down. Let your subconscious flow un-inhibited—don't worry about grammar. Write as if you were writing to a friend, instructing him or her on how to fully embrace that word/topic. What would you want the reader (you, in essence) to enjoy for that month?

Repeat this step for all twelve words/topics.

EXAMPLE: *Pick "Travel." Write a page of where you would like to travel, how you would like to travel, how would it enhance your life. Ask yourself—and write down the answer: Why is it important to you at this moment?*

Take a few days or even a week to complete this step. I usually write two to three letters per day. Have fun with this exercise and choose a place that feels good to sit and write. Go to your favorite coffee shop, your backyard, the beach, a library, a park. I like to write my letters on a vacation.

Step 5

☐ **Say "I love YOU."**

Leave enough room at the bottom of each page to sign off with the words "I love you." **Don't skip this step!** Even if it feels silly, write it. I promise that when you read the letter later on, it will feel good and start to feel normal.

Step 6

☐ **Gather twelve envelopes.**

After you have written one page about each of the twelve topics, fold the first page and place it inside an envelope (I like business-size envelopes; use whatever you prefer, just make sure they're all identical). Repeat this process with the remaining eleven pages and envelopes. Next, mix up all the envelopes, or have a friend mix them up for you.

Step 7

☐ Pick a date.

Now pick your favorite day of the month. My favorite number is nine, so for my first year of letters I picked the ninth day of each month. Once you've selected your number, write the date on the envelope according to that number for the coming year. For example, if you are reading this book in late March 2015, write "April 9, 2015" on the first envelope. On the second envelope, write "May 9, 2015." Continue writing the consecutive monthly date until all twelve envelopes have been dated.

Step 8

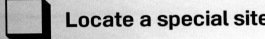 **Locate a special site.**

Find a special place in your home to store your monthly "gifts" to yourself. I chose a beautiful box that I found in Egypt and put the box on display in my bedroom.

Open a letter.

Every month, on that special date that you have picked, open the "gift" (letter) and read your monthly focus. Make a promise to yourself to fully concentrate on that specific topic and allow the focus to influence your activities and thoughts for the month. Take care to open the correct letter dated for that month. **Display the letter in a place where you can read it everyday.** Now enjoy! Trust that your inner guidance is already at work and influencing you through YOU.

EXAMPLE: If you opened the letter focusing on "Travel," listen to the advice/thoughts you wrote to yourself. Start to plan the travel you desire, look for inventive ways to travel to new places in your own city, travel the longer way home and enjoy the scenery, go camping. If someone asks you to do something regarding travel this month, take it as a sign and go!

Through this monthly guidance you will develop a relationship with yourself and cultivate an understanding of your soul's desires to live fully in this life.

"Trust that your
inner guidance is
already at work and
influencing you through
YOU."

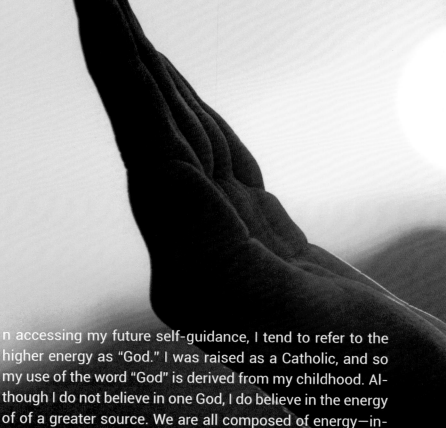

the greater
source

n accessing my future self-guidance, I tend to refer to the higher energy as "God." I was raised as a Catholic, and so my use of the word "God" is derived from my childhood. Although I do not believe in one God, I do believe in the energy of of a greater source. We are all composed of energy—influential matter that is possessed within our bodily form. The word "God" for me is also a description of self-awareness and intuition. When I wrote my first round of Life Letters,

I felt as though I were channeling a higher spiritual guidance. Whether it was that of my own or that of a celestial being, that is not something I care to judge. Rather, I encourage you to write from a safe place of inspiration. This source of inspiration should be called or referenced any way that makes you feel comfortable and open. Allow yourself the time to be inspired by the topic you have chosen. Allow yourself the openness to hear your "own" voice or that of your "God's" voice.

celebration

We have traditions as humans. Every New Year's Eve we count our blessings and misfortunes from the year before and embark on resolutions meant to bring ourselves closer to what we hope is greater happiness. We strive to make the biggest changes and challenge ourselves to the point of exhaustion. We make big plans, and, by the middle of the year, we feel depleted and/or have already given up. *Why?* Maybe the focus was too big and too broad. In my experience, no New Year's resolution has made it past the first few months of the year.

Life Letters has served me well for the past six years because it is a gift that keeps on giving for a full year. Each monthly letter allows me to be more specific about the growth I desire to make in my life. Each gives me the time to elaborate on what that idea/topic looks like to me. A month gives anyone enough time to not feel rushed, time to truly embrace that focus. Once I have concentrated on a letter's focus for the month, I find that whatever I've learned carries on with me. Then I continue onto the next month. *Life Letters* is a gift for the whole year!

> **"**
>
> ***Life Letters...* is an exciting approach to self-discovery with a greater perspective in fulfillment.**
>
> **"**

Life Letters is the gift of yourself to yourself to learn, live, love and grow. With Life Letters you have the liberty to freely live in the moment because your decisions for that month are concentrated on your focus topic. For example, one year I had a "Comedy" month, and so all my decisions were centered on that subject. When deciding what movie to go see, I knew it had to be a comedy. I looked up jokes online. I even attempted to write my own jokes. My focus was on comedy and laughter.

The timely structure of *Life Letters* helps give your life and desires a regular, monthly focus with a greater outcome for success. It is an exciting approach to self-discovery with a greater perspective in fulfillment. Go on, embrace your desires and love yourself to the greatest potential.

inspiration

Life Letters
enhances your life
with a focus on your soul's desire to
evolve.

October 9, 2009
"Happy / Thank You / More, Please"

You have been given so much this year and in your lifetime. This month you are going to break the self-sabotaging cycle and move the energy into helping others.

Happy Thank You More Please

The cycle never has to stop giving. Continue your practice of manifesting abundance and prosperity. But instead of the guilt you'd replace it with more generosity to those in need. This will continue the cycle of goodness coming your way and circling around to others.

Investigate areas that you thrive so that you may share your gifts with others.

At the end of each generous experience thank the person for allowing help and the connection to manifest positivity. Encourage that person to give a bit more to someone else. Now we've created a ripple. Collectively we are all responsible for change, help and love.

Give back and keep on receiving. This will be an impactful month.

I love you

October 12, 2012
"Knowledge / Brain Power"

Hello, my smart young lady. Over the course of the next 30 days you are going to be fixated on developing more of your brain. You live in a world where knowledge is at your finger tips and so much of your day is used not using all the talents of this vital organ.

So take the rest of the day to find a central area of focus for the month, maybe something that makes you go to the new beautiful Santa Monica Library. Just like school immerse yourself in research. Teach your brain whatever it lacks. Maybe begin to learn a new language as well. There is plenty of room to learn new things.

Your knowledge seeking will not stop there. Being aware of the world around you is power. Either watch one hour of the news everyday or take to reading the paper. Through these actions your conversations will evoke more knowledge. Seek out other people's knowledge or opinions. This will only formulate more this to research and develop more opinions for you to have on your new found knowledge. Enjoy you are exploring more talents of your being. Knowledge is power.

I love you.

February 5, 2010
"Yoga"

Yoga, breath and meditation.
Do you know who you truly are?
Could you stand in a room with
no materialistic defenses or words
and stand tall? What is standing
in the way of your true connection
to self?

This whole month is purely
about being with yourself for
at least an hour a day. 30 days
of breathing, stretching and
manifesting the greatest connection
of all - you.

Indulge in a daily yoga practice
that allows you to connect to
your fullest potential. You are
a true gift, give yourself the
time to enjoy that gift as well.
Practice your manifestations by
having a clear intention everyday
and be in gratitude for the
awareness and abundance that
you will be showered in!

This month is an experiment
in connecting your spirit to the
mind and body through breath
and enlightenment.

You are a light of love. Give
it energy to shine for yourself
as well as the world!

I love you!

October 9, 2012
"Nature"

all the colors, textures and energies of the world manifested beautifully in one place. Untouched by man, created through mysterious brilliance, and defying the odds of corruption... nature. Nature is the truest form of faith, patience, abundance, beauty and love.

This month you are invited to indulge in nature. Be one with nature. Model your lifestyle off of nature. Patience to grow through all seasons and obstacles. Faith to believe you are in the right place. Abundance to flourish in places that don't naturally make sense. Beauty of what has be given to you.

Each day start your day with moving meditation by walking through the neighborhood or hiking some new trails. Enjoy the ocean in all its wild behaviors. Camp under the stars. Vacation to Big Sur, Yosemite, the desert and embrace all that is around.

Thank you for the time to connect with the world around you. It will reward you with unmeasurable insight.

I love you.

June 9, 2013
"Girlfriends / Womanhood"

Embrace your womanhood. Look around you, your girlfriends are a mirror to your soul. How can you impact and truly immerse yourself into the love of your girlfriends?

Woman have the ability to multi-task, to change energy, to create life and to love unconditionally. A group of women can change each other in a positive or negative way... be that positive influence.

Share "circle of stones" with each of your girlfriends. Create various occassions this month for women to come together and be celebrated.

Strenghten each one of your relationships through sobering experiences. Book club, finance group, workout group, learning a new hobby group, laughing group, shopping group, sketch group... a girl's trip this month is a must. coordinate it at the beginning of the month.

Allow the women in your life to support you and give you the love you're so desperately missed.

And remember to celebrate each of their qualities. Enjoy being a woman.

I love you!

July 9, 2014
"Religion/Bible"

Seek to understand, then to be understood. There are many things that you don't understand, therefore cannot completely understand yourself or how you feel about it in your life. This month the focus is religion, what do you believe or understand and why you have general scholarly things around to inform you. Let's start with the basics. This month you will read the Bible from front to back, find your favorite quotes. Go to Bible study on Tuesday nights at Bel Air. Truly seek to understand your faith.

Also during this time take the luxury of exploring other religions or faiths. Read the history of God to understand the evolution of humans faith. Remember that you are human and we error on the side of judgement. Let your heart and God's word direct you towards your faith. Through this enlightment, strength and faith will emerge. Share with anyone who comes along, this is God's intention.

I love you.

May 5, 2010
"Creativity"

God has given you a talent, a gift to touch many of his children through your creative mind. From nothing he will give you the inspiration of thoughts to words, from nothing he will give you the experiences to feel all emotions, from love he will give you the purpose of your life. Your purpose is to live in God's intentions. Therefore have no fear of failure. Instead embrace your opportunities as a loving gift from him. Be thankful and fully present each time an opportunity presents itself - follow the light through the darkness. Your faith will shed light to many through your career. This month take every opportunity to study, to enhance your gift to be creative... write, act, follow your dream to influence the world. Imagine if your desire and will is this strong what could God's vision be because he is greater and thinks bigger than you ever could. Walk confidently towards your dreams knowing that God will place you on the right path. You will touch the lives of many through your craft. Just believe, ask and then you will succeed. Thank God for giving you the ability to live bigger than you could ever imagine.   I love you.

June 22, 2011
"Travel"

This is an exciting month for you, spending all your free time in unfamiliar grounds. You might already have some travel planned, so either this will accomodate the previous plans or you have lots of time to explore. Be creative so this does not drain the tank but also do not prohibit your experience by worrying about money. This trips can be short and around the area. Look where you are and why yate has it that you travel this month. Remember what you have learned from your past travels and secure the best for yourself. Maybe spend the majority of the time doing day trips all in California. Go to the San Diego Zoo by way of train, explore Napa Valley, Yosimeti, Seattle, Cornado Island, Lake Tahoe. Ask around and see who is up for the challenge of fun travels this month. But allow yourself to learn something new this month through your own eyes. Try one trip completely spontanously — see where the car takes you. Make some amazing CD's for the road and remember God is good company. I love you.

November 5, 2010
"Fun"

This month the whole month is focused on fun. Doing whatever makes you happiest at the moment. Laughter should fill your silence and reach to the bottom of your heart. Being so disciplined is a gift, allowing yourself to enjoy this world sometimes gets pushed aside because of the stress everyday. But your central focus for the month is to tap into your inner child. Play outside until it gets dark, go on many bike rides, see many comedy shows, only see funny movies, learn some jokes on your own, read a funny book (Chelsea Handler) have a game night. Completely surround yourself with people who make you laugh. Allow yourself to be completely free spirited let the laughter and true joy fill your mind so that with each passing day you will feel lighter. By the end of the month your body will crave fun just like it craves water. A smile will be the beginning of everyday as well as the goodnight kiss to yourself and remember to tell yourself every night how much you love this fun girl.

I love you!

'd like to thank all the brilliant people who came into my life and helped me to transfer the inspirational thoughts that were in my head to the pages you just read. First and foremost, I want to thank Suzanne Quast for joining me on both that wondrous hike up Egypt's Mt. Sinai and this journey of life. I want to thank Marnie Alton for creating a glorious space in her studio that allowed me to finish this book. Angela Davis, you are a leader of greatness—from your soul cycle class I learned that we are all "assigned to inspire," and I always ride in gratitude with you and for you. Which leads me to a guy named Tony, who decided one day to take Angela's 6 a.m. class. Tony, thank you for wearing *that T-shirt* (you know the one); it provided me with the final piece of the puzzle to finish my book. A huge thank you to Lisa Knight of DesignsDoneNow.com, who visually expressed my thoughts, helped me to design this book, answered this first-time writer's desperate questions, and introduced me to the lovely Lorna Corpus Sullivan. Lorna, thank you for helping me make my AP English teacher very proud. I want to thank Kate Hauschka for being a last-minute savior and producing stimulating photography. And my deepest gratitude to the first woman I ever met, Sherri Troyer, my mother. Mom, thank you for telling me each night of my childhood that I could do and be anything that I set my mind to and for writing my first biography. Thank you to my beautiful sister, Abigail Ochse, for being a constant source of support, my role model, and my biggest fan of anything weird and unusual that I try to do. Thank you to the great and wondrous "Hall of Famer" Bob Ochse, my dad, for his boundless love, support and advice (he thinks the fact that I can now say *I'm a published author* is pretty cool). And, while it might seem cheesy, I want to thank "the question mark in the sky." That question mark sent me on a road to discovering myself and opened my eyes to my friend Lee Knaz. Mr. Knaz, my now husband, I want to thank you for your everlasting words of support, unconditional love, encouragement and your bountiful insight—and for being so damn handsome.